DRA\
SPACES

Gareth Wynne

Thoughts from
a Damaged Mind

europe books

© 2021 **Europe Books** | London
www.europebooks.co.uk – info@europebooks.co.uk

ISBN 979-12-201-0857-7
First edition: April 2021

Distribution for the United Kingdom: **Vine House Distribution ltd**

Printed for Italy by Rotomail Italia
Finito di stampare nel mese di aprile 2021
presso Rotomail Italia S.p.A. - Vignate (MI)

Thoughts from a Damaged Mind

Above anyone else, I dedicate this book to my wife, Madeleine, without whom I would no longer be around.

I have walked a long, long way on a hazardous journey, and this book is also dedicated to those who have walked with me and to all those who walk their own perilous paths.

FOREWORD

Thoughts from a Damaged Mind is a poetic collection that narrates existentialism through the eyes of a unique and personal experience. With words that are familiar to every reader's ordinary life, the poet often describes a deep, acute feeling of isolation and estrangement towards the societal norms through which people are bound to be considered sane, whole, and normal. What makes a person normal? What makes a person acceptable to the society we live in? It is worth it, to be normal in order to be accepted? Does the word *normal* even have a meaning or is it just a set of superficial, empty, meaningless, and socially accepted behaviors? The poet interrogates himself on these questions, as an inner dark and unwelcomed guest seems to take over every feeling of joy and passion, but, above all, it seems to prevent the poet's individuality to manifest into the open.

Depression, the unwelcomed guest, is often a misunderstood one. Too many people proclaim without the shadow of a doubt that they are depressed because they feel sad, they feel frustrated, or hurt, not knowing the difference between an intense but temporary feeling and an illness. Depression itself is not painful, but rather the opposite: it is the absence of pain. But it is also the absence of happiness. The absence of inspiration. The absence of enthusiasm. The absence of dreams. The absence of any feeling at all. It slowly devours one's individuality, until the only feeling left is that of a shell with the memories of a far, previous life. And that is painful. Depression is what prevents a person from living the "ups and downs or downs and ups" of life, a locked prison of incommunicability, a horrendous "personal Hell".

When not given an incorrect and shallow meaning, depression is often stigmatized. It is not yet commonly accepted by the majority of people that a human mind can fall ill just like the body, regardless of one's strength, wit, or determination. Instead of receiving the support that any unwell person is entitled to, the ones suffering from depression are often bound to hear, "Stay strong," or "Try harder!" Maybe the most important message conveyed by *Thoughts from a Damaged Mind* is this: it could happen to anyone. And we are reminded of it at every line. The poet has friends, an amazing wife, lives in a lovely country, he is a dog lover. The poet could be your neighbor or coworker. Could be your best friend. Your child. You.

The acceptance of depression as an illness, not only from the patient but also from the patient's family and friends, is maybe the first step to putting a stop to the walls of incommunicability and loneliness that must be demolished to start a path towards recovery. The acceptance and acknowledgment of reality, along with what reality brings – the help of a loved one, the care of a doctor, even the warmth of the sun – are the roots of the one thing that is never lost: hope.

AUTHOR'S NOTE

I am a retired police officer who was diagnosed with depression in January 2014. I was subsequently sectioned to the care of a local psychiatric hospital where I remained for just over two weeks. My early experiences of mental health services were poor in the extreme, the consequences of which had a devastating and lasting impact on my mental health and on the course of my life. Consequently, in addition to the depression, I am now diagnosed with Complex PTSD and anxiety.

A hat trick, you might say.

When released, I lived with my present wife, Madeleine, who is responsible for my ongoing survival.

Since July 2015, when we moved to Dorset, I have received excellent treatment and care from dedicated, talented professionals with the ability to recognise the harm that had already been done.

Together, they showed me how to trust once again and gave me the resources and confidence to recover from that harm.

The poetry in this book is based on my experiences and ongoing struggle with my mental ill-health. There are also some poems that relate to past situations that I believe had a profound and detrimental effect on me.

I just want to add that we all have to take care of our mental health, just as we have to take care of our physical health. Due to my circumstances, I have poor mental health. I feel that there is still a stigma surrounding the issue. There is no good reason for this. What happened to me could happen to anyone. Fortunately, I now have a supportive wife in Madeleine, who tries to keep me on the straight and narrow and I owe her so much.

A life all alone
With a wife at home.
My head such a mess
While under duress,
Longing for death
To breathe my last breath.
Stuck in a crazy world
Where everything unfurled.

A life full of peace,
Full of hope and release;
A head clear and calm,
Protect me from harm;
A happy and glorious wife
With whom to share my life.

Two worlds that collide
And fight for control of my life.
Who knows the victorious side?
Who knows what happens to my life?

Working With Love

The working day can be a drag
Feeling remote and bored.
What you are doing is not your bag,
Wondering what life has in store.

Working with dogs and cats
Is never the same;
Your day with them helps you to relax
As all of the animals are glad you came.

The people who work there
All love cats and dogs.
There's nothing elsewhere
Comes close to drive those cogs.

Remember they work there,
Thank heavens above,
That they care
And shower your pets with love.

What Is a Life?

Life is for living
Or so they say.
But what if it's giving
Nothing but pain?

Should you go on
Till it all starts to change?
Or lie back and let it all be gone?
Or maybe I'm just deranged?

Choices are hard;
When you are unsure
Just pick a card:
The choice is the cure.

For what is a life?
Just moving through time,
Cutting away like a sharp-bladed knife
Till all that is left is...

Time

Time moves on
But my life stands still.
Am I the only one
Still taking this pill?

To give up is easy
But life gets in the way.
Thoughts won't let me be
They try to take my will away.

The people at Merley
Insist it takes time.
This makes it sound easy,
They are not in my mind.

Have I got time?
Will it run out
Before I get right?
Maybe it's already some doubt.

Time is against me,
A really tough fight.
What will this result be?
Who knows?

Three Little Words

Three little words that we use
So much.

They are spoken so many times
Without real thought.

Their potency is really such

That they should only be used
With care.

Their meaning can become so bland
When used so often they become quite bare,

While on the other hand,
When said and thought right through,

Those three little words alone can stand,
Three little words, "I love you."

The First Night

"Lights Out!"
I hear the shout.
The door slams with a heavy clang.
Alone in the silence,
Then a bang,
And yet more noise.
Just silence.
Alone on your bunk,
Dave up above,
He farts and snores and sleeps.
Frightened and all alone,
I feel the tears run down my face.
Dave just farts and snores and sleeps.
I cannot let him know I weep,
Scared and all alone.
Noise always
But silence
Terrified and all alone
All alone.

Thirty-two Years

Thirty-two years,
Give or take.
So many tears
My heart to break.

All of the lies
She told to me,
Rise up to the skies
And set me free.

Now I can love
And enjoy life.
Thank Heaven above
For my gorgeous wife

Strangers

Strangers can become friends,
You just have to let them in.
Take a chance on how it ends;
Don't consign them to the bin.

Everybody needs a friend
To engage with and show they care,
To give out and to send
And knowing that they're there.

So take a look around
And see what you can find,
Lonely people do abound
Don't leave them all behind.

Just take a little time
And stop and share a word.
Responses can be sublime
As now a friend is heard.

Questions

We all ask the questions
Talking in all of the sessions
We're left in a quandary
Not sure of our memory.

Thought things were better
Than just being treated as from the gutter,
What did I do or not do
To be hurt so much by you?

Those questions I ask
But I'm stuck in an impasse.
The pain is so great,
But still I await

The answers to all
The hard questions.

Ode to a Pea Fritter

Throughout our culinary land
Strange, unusual foods appeal.
They unite the local band
Of people who seem sincere.

Now, mushy peas are a must
With fish and chips, of course.
They make the meal robust,
Nothing can compare, of which there can be no discourse.

In strange and wild Dorsetshire
There's something we feel quite bitter.
I know not how it did transpire
That oddball called a pea fritter.

I've tried some strange concoctions
I never was a quitter
'Till I tried that weird invention
They call a pea fritter.

Madness

Madness is such a strange concept.
What it is, is hard to define.
We are never sure what to expect;
The stock answer is that we're fine.

There are many types of insanity,
Supposedly experienced by one in four,
Hard to admit because of our vanity
Far better to keep shut the door.

I know that I'm mad
But why should I care?
I know I'm not bad,
I'm just not all there.

People cannot understand.
They consider us strange.
Maybe they're so grand
But frightened of change.

We are not mad or strange
Just different in such a wide range.

I Am not Mad

I am not mad.
They are all mad.
I walk around
Not following the crowd.

I dress with passion
Not following the fashion.
I choose what I do
Not what I'm told to do.

I have my own ideas
Not getting them from social media.
I have real friends
Not Facebook friends.

I live as I please
Not always trying to appease.
Our lives are to lead,
Not follow like sheep.

Others are all part of the mass
Being different, I am seen as mad.

Happiness

Happiness. How do we define it?
Is it walking around grinning all day?
Or laughing and joking along the way?
Could it be money stored in a bank?
Or having high status or public rank?

It is looking at the one you love,
Knowing you fit like a hand in a glove.
You know they will always be there,
That no matter what, they will always care.

It's waking up and feeling their warmth
Loving when you're a grump
And buying things for them from the dump.

You know that they're the reason
You're alive,
That they give you a reason to survive,
To always be with the one you love,
Madeleine. My one and only true love.

Forgotten

A quiet dark lonely road,
The man is all alone.
He bears such a heavy load
While slowly heading home.

His wife and his daughter wait
Eager to welcome him home.
He opens the door passed the gate
And kisses and hugs his joyous welcome.

After dinner, he feels a tickle
But forgets while watching TV,
Where he feels he deserves a tipple
Before heading upstairs to sleep.

Morning sounds with a lark
And slowly they all awake
To find the tickle has become a bark
And now he starts to bake.

As he then self isolates,
Daughter begins to bark.
He realises it's too late
His wife is slow off the mark.

Before the evening has turned to dark,
All three are locked inside.
Finally, his wife does bark
Making it family wide.

They isolate as a family
Left to their own devices.
It's amazing how easily
No one misses the Prices.

One month later, as things calm down,
Friends and neighbours realise,
With questions and furrowed brow.
Eventually they find the Prices

Alone at home all were ill
No one thought nor dread
The Prices cuddled together still
Were now all sadly dead.

Five Years

Five long years
So many tears.
All of those lies
Without any real goodbyes.

A lying, devious bitch,
Who really belongs in a ditch,
Scheming and cheating so much
Surprising me out of touch.

Belief in so much lost
At such a terrible cost,
Cancelling all of my days
And leaving me in a haze.

Damaged by West Mercia,
Who knows why?
They acted so wrong and peculiar
And took on such a lie.

Justice, I'm sure, will come,
But I don't know when it will be done.
Time has run out for me.
The suffering continues unceasingly.

Now that my time has come,
I'll do what must be done.
Those bastards, West Mercia,
Have led to this hysteria.

Dogs

A dog is a friend,
There is no doubt.
Staying with you right to the end
Stuck to you throughout,

No matter how they are treated:
Whether very well or bad,
They never feel cheated
And never get mad.

They make you happy when you are sad,
There, by your side, for you,
They are there to make your heart feel good
Cheering you up no matter how blue.

A wag of a tail,
A nudge and a shove,
They never will fail
To show you their love.

Depression

Depression is such an overused word
People use it when they feel down.
Depression is so much more:
Depression will grind you to the ground.

Depression takes your heart and soul,
It makes your life a mess.
You wonder if again you can be well
Or is this all that's left?

A song says suicide is painless,
As if we really care.
Anything to stop this distress
That we are unable to share.

Another song says the drugs don't work
But I think they keep me well.
If you listen to me talk
You know they help to survive my
Private hell.

I don't know what the future holds
While gripped by this evil thing
I have to try to fight to get old
Otherwise, it feels I've given in.

Depressed

More and more are getting depressed
That's what they tell us in the press.
Perhaps they've done some kind of test,
Maybe we should all be impressed?

I think the rise is clearly obvious,
Depression must be contagious.
I think it is really outrageous
That has seen this still infectious.

It just needs a strong will
For us to have a little pill
To protect us from the brain's ills
But we are waiting still.

Brexit

"Brexit, Brexit," is all we hear;
Let's not forget Project Fear.
Of course, we have to note
That we have already had our vote.

Cameron put it all in play
Then he went and ran away
Theresa picked up the ball
Now it looks like we're heading for a fall.

What is up with the politicians?
They can't seem to make decisions.
Perhaps it's time for someone to say,
"To hell with it all, we're going to stay!"

A Brand New Life

Life begins at forty,
Or so I've heard,
But I am sixty,
Don't say a word.

My life has just begun,
I know I'm late,
I always was one
To hesitate.

A brand new start
Is what I have;
An open heart
That is now safe;

A loving wife
To share it all.
A brand new life
Just hear my call.

A Flat Life

Life is full of ups and downs
Or is it downs and ups?
Who knows?
Is there a difference?
But life is never flat.

We have to live with the ups and downs
Or downs and ups.
Whichever you choose,
A flat life never works.

Enjoy life's ups and down
Or downs and ups,
As they bring variety
And make life worth living.
Don't have a flat life.

A House

There's a magical, mysterious house
All private and somewhat subdued
Staff waiting inside, ready to pounce
And deal with all that's arrived.

Paula's the chief architect,
Controlling it all with aplomb.
Another on whom we reflect
Goes under the name of Tom.

Then there, of course, is Adele,
Laughing and smiling all day.
Rob waits around for to tell
Where we will go out to play.

Christy explains our life skills
While keeping our feet on the ground.

A light

I see a light
So far away.
It shines so bright,
What does it say?

Is it Death?
Or is it Life?
I hold my breath
With inner strife.

It leads the way
I know not where.
I cannot stay,
Of that I'm sure.

I need that light
To help me roam,
I hope it might
Take me home.

A Pink Rabbit

A pink rabbit just sits and waits,
Chaotic life surrounds him,
Dogs all licking plates
He just takes it all in.

Life for him is good,
Keeping nice and warm
No hiding in the mud.
For him, life is calm.

Chuckling away,
A grin upon his face,
While all the others play
He just keeps his place.

A Single Crack

A single crack.
I feel the wet
And cling on to the child.
The cries they rise and swell.
A flash of black
And then a scream.
The child cries louder;
I close my eyes.
Welcome to my private Hell.

Back to Being Whole

We live our lives
Following the rules,
Keeping in line.
But who are the fools

To go along
With everyone
Only to believe
To be as one?

If only to be free
And break the norm
How would that be?
Like being reborn.

That is the future
To take back control
To shun that, you're
Back to being whole.

Black and Red

Black is the night,
White is the day.
Where is the light?
Hiding away.

Red is the blood
Which flows from the cut
And seeps in the wood
While eyes slowly shut.

Black

Black is dark and dark is
Black.

We try to hide these thoughts
Back;

These thoughts are always
There,

We try to keep them in the
Air.
.
Death is trying to have its
Way,

That's why you fight every
Day.

The win is worse, but you can't
Lose.

Death sounds good, as it
Would

Harder to stay alive, but that must
Be your only drive.

Cold

A frosty, moonlit night
Frost crunching underfoot
Thankful for the light
Walking with just one thought.

A rucksack on his back
Loaded with all he needs,
Warm clothing upon his back,
Clear about the night's deeds.

He stumbles when on rough ground,
Still purposeful, on he goes
With silence all around.
His pace never falters or slows.

At last, he has got to where
He intends to breathe his last.
He pauses to stop and stare
Thinking about his past.

He reaches a wooden pier
Empties his rucksack,
So sure now that he is here
There can be no turning back.

He sits on the cold, damp wood
Lowers his feet in the water,
A feeling so cold, but good
Like a lamb heading for slaughter.

A drink from a flask of coffee,
The warmth flowing through him,
He opens his bottle of whisky
And fumbles his pills so slim.

Mixing the whisky and coffee,
Taking the pills one by one,
Feeling so calm and free
He smokes a cigar 'till it's done.

His letters are in the rucksack;
Three he has written in total.
He knows there is no turning back
As the whisky and coffee take their toll.

He begins to feel quite sleepy
Despite all of the cold
He starts to slowly weep
As he lays down on the wood so cold.

His eyes close to the night,
The end is getting near.
The beautiful silence is right
As he gently slips away from here.

Dog Love

Barney, Max, Khan, Monty, and Stan
Five lovely dogs, but all so different.
Shep, Rex, Jett, and Dillon
Four who belong to special moments.

Only Jett and Dillon now remain
But the others are so locked in my brain.
The love that all dogs show
Can leave you all aglow.

To live without a dog is so wrong;
They all give so much more than they take.
They love you even when you're not feeling strong
And snuggle up while you're away.

They guard us,
They guide us,
They love us.
We who know them live with a bonus.

E. O. P.

I live in a lovely Country
With lots of nice people to meet
And everyone is free
With plenty of things to eat.

The life we lead is good
And everyone is happy
Just as they should
Where life is as it should be.

Strange things happened down the road,
Things so unexpected, causing unease.
People began to explode
When they became obese.

A lesson is there to be learned:
Enjoy your life and food.
Remember time bombs are earned
So think of being good.

Falling

Falling, falling, falling.
It feels so free. Like flying.
Surrounded by darkness,
How long is this caress?

Seems to fall forever.
Time has gone altogether
I wait 'till I can feel the end
But I wait for what I intend.

Suddenly,
That's it.
No more,
No pain.

Just silence and peace.

Flying

I'm flying:
A great feeling.
Now I'm smiling,
Free at last.

I feel the wind
As it rushes past.
All is quiet
But it won't last.

No more worries,
No more cares,
No more dodgy curries,
Or gummy bears.

Peace at last.
Grinning all the way,
Going so fast,
But only one...

Flight terminated.

Heads

We all have a head
That has thoughts, which are hidden.
We may wish that we are dead;
These thoughts don't see the light of day.

Some may say we are crazy
Or going out of our mind,
Maybe even mad?
I'd rather be mad than out of my mind.

Help

When your head is going wrong
You cannot wait alone too long.
Hahnemann House can keep you strong;
They keep you singing the same song.

As you work on getting well
To keep you from your personal Hell
You listen and can have a chat
With others who are feeling flat.

We ask each other, "How is it for you?"
While we are still feeling blue.
Trying hard to smile and play,
We are making it through another day.

All of this help is so great,
Maybe we should celebrate?
The Dorset CMHT provide
A service that is full of pride.

I Am not a Number

Our lives are governed by numbers
They define who we are.

2460, 8068, 4043,
We can't live without them.

They control our health
And our wealth.

They dictate what we buy
And though we may try.

They take over our lives,
They don't want your name.

Just your number,
So many to remember.

I am not a number;
I am a free man.

Lost

Strange buildings all around,
People talking,
Strange sounds.
I keep on walking.

I am lost,
Looking for home,
I know not where
Or how to find my home.

I hear laughter,
People having fun,
I'm not sure what I'm after
But I start to run.

I don't understand;
What is going on?
In this strange, foreign land
I am scared, but carry on.

I see no signs
Of places I know,
There are no lines
 For me to follow.

People stop and stare,
I don't know why
And I don't care.
I just sigh.

Where is home?
I need to know
How long must I roam?
'Till safe at home.

Mind

Jumble, life, death, bitch
Love, man, hate, fear, lust
Sex, nurse, bride, hell, rich
Joy, light, angst, cash, bust
Heaven, sun, hair, hanging, blood
Dead, splat, pain, fat, black
Train, plane, sea, earth, mud
Slash, boat, pills, beach, crack
Fall, home, left, devil, why
Sky, drown, kill, work, write
Son, sink, drug, full, sigh
Fuck, joke, sad, foul, bite
Kick, fall, scare, sing
Razor, heart, whisky, dead
Cut, bleed, dead, run, tread
Dead, gas, lynch, dead, dead
Hope, dead, feel, dead, life, dead
Dead, love, dead, dead, brief, dead
Dead, dead, dead, calm, dead, dead
Dead, dead, dead, dead, dead, release
Relief.

My Love, My Life

Blonde hair gently framing
A pale, kind face;
Brown eyes kindly watching
A gentle smile lights the room.

Tiny of frame
But strong of heart,
Strength emanating, regardless of size,
Comfort to be found in those loving arms.

Love is so hard for her,
Life has been cruel.
Now she is safe
From life's savages and pain.

A man who loves her
Unconditional, in totality,
To love her as she deserves
And keep her safe from harm.

Numbers

2460, 8368, 2607, 1957, 2015,
Numbers. We live by numbers.

BH31, 2000, 1970, 2007, 1977,
Numbers are everywhere.

0703, 0108, 2023, 0502,
They rule everything.

Algorithms are the new God,
2607, 8368, 2023, 1970.

Everything dictated by numbers:
Whether we have children,

How much we earn,
Where we live,

Whether we live or DIE.

Pain

Every day I feel the pain.
I think I'm going insane.
Perhaps I'll take some pills
To take away my ills,

Or walk into the sea
On some deserted beach,
Or somewhere nice and tall
Where I can take a fall,

Or maybe a sharp knife
To cut away this life.
For who would really care
If I wasn't there?

Passing Him by

Why is life so shit?
Why do I experience such crap?
Surely this cannot be it?
Always getting a slap.

Shit just keeps on happening
To those who don't deserve it.
There's no point complaining
No-one hears one bit.

Happiness is all too brief,
Then kicks us in the teeth.
Nothing good lasts long,
Just what have we done wrong?

Some believe in a God;
I cannot understand why.
God seems a real cruel sod;
I think I'll pass Him by.

Potholes

I hate school holidays.
They fill me with such malaise,

Those days of endless dreams
Where nothing is as it seems.

Thoughts cause such unrest
Not knowing what is best.

My life just seems to drag,
Pleasure locked away in bags.

Hope is all I have
That some day it will all repave

The potholes
Left in my soul.

Stand up for Yourself

There are times in life
When decisions must be made;
Living in constant strife
Or stepping up to make the grade?

None of this is easy
But to make life more fun
Making it all so much more breezy
Though it has to be done.

So time to make your mark
Stand up for yourself;
Not just for the lark
No more sitting on the shelf.

The Special Ones

So tired of it all
But not sleepy.
We're wide awake,
Relax and chill.

Lovely Madeleine,
The one who kept me sane,
My love for her is very special
I wish I'd known her long ago.

What about Sharon?
Helped me carry on.
A very special lady
Always there to rely on.

Then there's Dr. K,
Who really is okay.
She really does care
Though we're not always aware.

They all swirl round in my head,
Making me smile.
They were all so kind
Over such a short while.

What of Sam or Seb?

I look up to the skies
Feel the heaviness of my eyes.

Sleep is coming at last
All my troubles are in the past.

A final sigh,
A broad smile,
A final breath,
So this is Death.

Telephone

I'm sitting staring at the telephone.
I'm feeling so alone
Waiting for it to ring
And all the joy that it would bring.

But it remains silent
Feeling the pain that it has sent,
Pondering where I went wrong,
Not to have him sing a sweet song.

I tried my best as he grew up
But obviously failed with my young pup.
I think of times we spent alone
While staring at the telephone.

The Value of Your Life

We take our life
With ne'er a thought
To end the strife
That we have wrought.

It's sometimes hard
To carry on;
You deal Death's cards
From the deck of one.

You have to fight,
Just to keep going
To see the light
That shows you're growing.

The help you get
From CMHT and wife
They help to set
The value of your life.

What Comes Next?

What comes next?
We often ask.
Almost like a reflex
Is kept behind a mask.

What if there is nothing?
No Allah, God,
Not anything.
Just the earthly sod.

We need to have some drive
Rather than enjoy what comes.
It's surely good to be alive?
Relax and enjoy some sun.

Until the Very Last Day

An evening in the Bistro
The food was good,
The wine did flow,
Conversations were low.

A wrong word was said,
No harm meant,
But the air turned red
So the bill was paid.

Out into the night,
Into the cold,
Harsh words came with might
Platitudes met with slight.

Into the home
No thoughts of peace.
Like gladiators in Rome
Words like daggers were thrown.

A punch was thrown
Into a face;
A punch was thrown,
A wall hit alone.

Nothing was said
Off up the stairs.
Both went to bed
Separate rooms taken as read.

The happy couple on holiday
Life will go on
When even away,
Until the very last day.

What's Inside?

As I walk the street
The people that I meet
They do not know
'Cause it does not show.

But I must confess
That my head's a mess,
If they only caught
Some of my thoughts.

For it's a fact
They may react
Although I cannot see
If they're the same as me.

For I'm only one in four,
So there must be more,
But we all hide
The thoughts inside.

And that we are scared
That nobody cares.

Why?

A man marries a woman. Why?
A son gets born. Why?
The woman is abusive. Why?
The man suffers in silence. Why?
The woman hurts the man. Why?
The man falls apart. Why?
The police arrest the man. Why?
They send the man to prison. Why?
No case to answer. Why?
The son chooses the woman. Why?
Now the man is broke. Why?
There is no justice. Why?
Life carries on. Why?
Or maybe not. Why?
The hardest question is why.
So hard to comprehend why.
Stuck in the head. Why?
Please explain why.

Index

9   Foreword

11   Author's Note

13   Worlds at War

14   Working With Love

15   What Is a Life?

16   Time

17   Three Little Words

18   The First Night

19   Thirty-two Years

20   Strangers

21   Questions

22   Ode to a Pea Fritter

23   Madness

24   I Am not Mad

25   Happiness

26   Forgotten

28   Five Years

29   Dogs

30   Depression

31   Depressed

32   Brexit

33   A Brand New Life

34   A Flat Life

35   A House

36   A light

37	A Pink Rabbit
38	A Single Crack
39	Back to Being Whole
40	Black and Red
41	Black
42	Cold
44	Dog Love
45	E. O. P.
46	Falling
47	Flying
48	Heads
49	Help
50	I Am not a Number
51	Lost
53	Mind
54	My Love, My Life
55	Numbers
56	Pain
57	Passing Him by
58	Potholes
59	Stand up for Yourself
60	The Special Ones
62	Telephone
63	The Value of Your Life
64	What Comes Next?
65	Until the Very Last Day
67	What's Inside?
68	Why?